"Most Christians know we should care for one another. But few of us know how. Seasoned biblical counselor and author Ed Welch not only gifts us with the *how* but, like a great chef, serves it up in eight concise, biblically true, and richly wise courses. Each brief chapter can be read aloud to a group and is accompanied by heart-piercing, eye-opening discussion questions. This is a book that can shape the culture of our churches to be safe places of wise mutual care. I heartily recommend it!"

Alfred J. Poirier, Visiting Professor in Practical Theology, Westminster Theological Seminary, Glenside, PA; author, *The Peacemaking Pastor*

"Nearly every Christian has experienced awkwardness in the local church. At one time or another, we have felt ignored, misunderstood, or out of place. The church may be the body of Christ, but we don't always function as well as we should. In *Caring for One Another*, Ed Welch gives us thoroughly biblical and entirely practical direction to facilitate more meaningful interactions in our churches. In the space of eight short lessons, we learn our need to move toward people and find ourselves equipped to reach out to them in loving and genuinely helpful ways. Whether you read this book alone or study it in a group, you will close the last page with renewed energy for building relationships in your church."

Megan Hill, author, *Praying Together*; Editor, The Gospel Coalition; Editorial Board Member, *Christianity Today*

"One of God's chosen ways to help people is through the care and concern of fellow Christians. In our busy world with its superficial relationships, many have abandoned this calling and left it to professionals to do the work ordinary Christians could be doing to help others. Through easy-to-follow practical guidelines, Ed Welch shows how we can remedy this and make our churches into caring communities. This kind of caring can be a means God uses not only to bless Christians but also to commend the Christian way to those outside the church."

Ajith Fernando, Teaching Director, Youth for Christ, Sri Lanka; author, *The Call to Joy and Pain*

"This is a short book, but one that packs a powerful punch. Ed Welch has given us a user-friendly guide for our churches to grow together as we seek to better care for one another. I love that the lessons are meant to be read aloud and discussed among church members. I'm already envisioning various groups of people I can read this book with in our congregation. Buy this book. Better yet, buy a case of books to pass out in your church. And even better than that, get people within your church reading it together. The impact of this book could have far-reaching effects in our churches as we seek to love one another in a way that shines the spotlight on Christ."

Dave Furman, Senior Pastor, Redeemer Church of Dubai; author, *Kiss the Wave* and *Being There*

"*Caring for One Another* is a concise guide for helping others. It contains gems of biblical wisdom and sound principles, encouraging readers to move toward others with all humility, to be personal and pray, and to sensitively talk about suffering and sin. I highly recommend this very helpful book to all Christians."

Siang-Yang Tan, Professor of Psychology, Fuller Theological Seminary; Senior Pastor, First Evangelical Church Glendale, CA; author, *Counseling and Psychotherapy: A Christian Perspective*

"Short, biblical, practical, wise—if you need help building meaningful relationships, Ed Welch will be your perfect guide. *Caring for One Another* will be a must-read for everyone I train."

Deepak Reju, Pastor of Biblical Counseling and Family Ministry, Capitol Hill Baptist Church, Washington, DC; author, *The Pastor and Counseling* and *She's Got the Wrong Guy*

"I need this book. My church needs this book. My local community needs my church to read this book. Ed Welch envisions a new kind of caring community that walks in dependence on the grace of God. With Christ-centered love and wisdom, he shows us what it looks like and how we can get there. I want this for my family, for my church, and for the glory of God. When it comes to caring for others, this is the first book I will reach for to stir my soul, shape my prayers, and train my church."

Ste Casey, Course Tutor and Speaker, Biblical Counselling UK; Pastor, Speke Baptist Church, Liverpool, England

Caring for
One Another

Caring for One Another

8 Ways to Cultivate
Meaningful Relationships

Edward T. Welch

WHEATON, ILLINOIS

Trade paperback ISBN: 978-1-4335-6109-2
ePub ISBN: 978-1-4335-6112-2
PDF ISBN: 978-1-4335-6110-8
Mobipocket ISBN: 978-1-4335-6111-5

Library of Congress Cataloging-in-Publication Data

Names: Welch, Edward T., 1953- author.
Title: Caring for one another : 8 ways to cultivate meaningful relationships / Ed Welch.
Description: Wheaton : Crossway, 2018. | Includes bibliographical references and index.
Identifiers: LCCN 2017054426 (print) | LCCN 2018004806 (ebook) | ISBN 9781433561108 (pdf) | ISBN 9781433561115 (mobi) | ISBN 9781433561122 (epub) | ISBN 9781433561092 (tp)
Subjects: LCSH: Interpersonal relations–Religious aspects–Christianity. | Caring–Religious aspects–Christianity.
Classification: LCC BV4597.52 (ebook) | LCC BV4597.52 .W445 2018 (print) | DDC 248.4–dc23
LC record available at https://lccn.loc.gov/2017054426

Crossway is a publishing ministry of Good News Publishers.

LB		29	28	27	26	25	24	23	22	21	20	19
15	14	13	12	11	10	9	8	7	6	5	4	

Contents

Preface

Our *calling* is to care for each other's souls. We want to bring our struggles to the Lord and to each other so that the church can be strengthened and the world can witness wisdom and love.

But since we have a long list of our own problems, we could easily think that care for others is best left to those who are more qualified. But the kingdom of God operates in ways we might not expect. Here, the humble and weak are the ones who do the heavy lifting of pastoral care:

> [Jesus] gave the apostles, the prophets, the evangelists, the shepherds and teachers, to equip the saints for the work of ministry, for building up the body of Christ, until we all attain to the unity of the faith and of the knowledge of the Son of God, to mature manhood, to the measure of the stature of the fullness of Christ. (Eph. 4:11–13)

Shepherds and teachers do the work of ministry. They also train us to do the work of ministry. Apparently, the

Lord is pleased to use ordinary people, through seemingly ordinary acts of love, to be the prime contributors to the maturing of his people. If you have trusted in Jesus rather than yourself, and you feel weak and unqualified, then you are qualified. Then you are *called*.

The goal of these eight lessons is to further shape the culture of your church so that counseling and mutual care of souls become natural features of the body's everyday life. The lessons are short but dense with essential theology and teeming with possible applications. They are intended to be read aloud in a group (participants don't have to read anything beforehand).

Lesson 1

With All Humility

Our helpfulness—our care for souls—starts with our *need* for care. We need God, and we need other people. Maturity through dependence is our goal. As a way to put this humility to the test, we ask for prayer. This will contribute to a church culture that is less self-protective and more united.

Imagine—an interconnected group of people who entrust themselves to each other. You can speak of your pain, and someone responds with compassion and prayer. You can speak of your joys, and someone shares in them with you. You can even ask for help with sinful struggles, and someone prays with you, offers hope and encouragement from Scripture, and sticks with you until sin no longer seems to have the upper hand. There is openness, freedom, friendship, bearing burdens together, and giving and receiving wisdom. No trite responses. And Jesus is throughout it all.

We want more of this.

As we come to Jesus, he has forgiven and washed us so that we can speak openly without shame, he has loved us so that we can love him and others freely, and he has given us wisdom and power from his Spirit so that we can help each other in ways that build up and give hope. In his honor and in his strength we want to grow into a wonderfully interdependent, wise, loving body of Christ—one in which we can help each other in times of trouble.

The Apostle Paul Makes Humility a Priority

In Ephesians 3, Paul actually prayed that we would be this kind of community (vv. 14–21). He also taught us how to do it:

> I therefore, a prisoner for the Lord, urge you to walk in a manner worthy of the calling to which you have been called, *with all humility and gentleness, with patience*, bearing with one another in love, eager to maintain the unity of the Spirit in the bond of peace. (Eph. 4:1–3)

Augustine wrote, "That first way [to truth] is humility; the second way is humility, and the third way is humility."[1] If humility does not precede our wisdom and help, our efforts are meaningless. Paul, it seems, would agree. Life in Christ starts with humility.

Humility simply acknowledges our many sins and limitations, and it responds with, "I need Jesus, and I need other people." It is an attractive package that includes trust in God's control, confidence in the Lord's forgiveness and love, and an openness that comes not from having to *be* someone but from resting in Jesus. It turns out that the simple acknowledgment of our neediness and weakness opens a door to the grace of God where we find confidence, peace, security, wisdom, strength, and freedom in him.

Humility Leads to Prayer

One way to put humility to work is this: ask someone to pray for you. God has established his kingdom on earth in such a way that we must ask for help. We ask the Lord for help, and we ask other people. Until we see him face-to-face, God works through his Spirit and his people.

It only *sounds* simple. It is one thing to ask the Lord for help. Even if our faith is especially weak, we have heard that he invites and hears our cries for help (Ps. 62:8), and we are willing to risk a little openness before him. It is something much different to ask a friend. Our pride resists being vulnerable. Even more, if you have ever confided in someone and received comments that were hurtful or less than supportive, you might have decided on the spot never to let that happen again, which means that you keep your troubles to yourself. This self-protective strategy might seem effective in the short run. It is not, however, how God created us to be with each other, so it will eventually lead to misery rather than safety. We opt instead for a better way. The process of asking for prayer is outlined below.

1. *Identify Trouble in Your Life*

Trouble is always knocking at the door. The list of troubles usually includes money, work, relationships, health, and matters specifically connected to our knowledge of Jesus and how to live for and with him.

2. *Connect a Particular Trouble with Scripture*

When you connect your troubles with Scripture, you are joining your life to the promises, graces, and commands of God. It takes time to develop this skill because there is so much Scripture, but you probably have the gist of what God says:

"Sometimes I find it hard to even pray for difficult things in my life. Would you pray that I know—deeply, in my heart—that God cares and invites me to pour out my heart to him?" (Ps. 62:8)

"I have been sick for a while and can get so discouraged. Could you pray that I would be able to turn quickly to Jesus when I feel especially miserable?" (2 Cor. 4:16–18)

"I have been snippy with my spouse over the last few weeks. Could you pray that I live with humility and gentleness as we try to talk about difficult things together?" (Eph. 4:1)

"I have been so frustrated with my daughter to the point where I want respect more than I want to be patient and show kindness to her. Could you pray for me?" (1 Cor. 13:4)

"My department manager has been critical and gruff recently. I don't know how to even think about this. Do you have any ideas on how I could pray?" (Rom. 12:18)

If you don't know how to pray, ask others to help you make the connections between your needs and God's Word.

It is God's will that we say "help" both to him and to others. As we do, we will take an important step toward being able to help others, since needy, humble helpers are the best helpers. And along the way, we will bless our community and induce others toward being needy, open, and vulnerable.

Discussion and Response

1. Have you ever asked another person to pray for you? How did it go?

2. Practice making the connection between your needs and God's promises. If possible, identify specific Scripture, but that isn't necessary to begin. You could practice with your own needs or use scenarios such as these:

   - Health concerns

   - Financial fears

   - Relationship difficulties

3. How do you hope to grow in being needy? Who might you ask to pray for you?

4. Take time to pray together.

Lesson 2

Move toward Others

God takes the initiative and moves toward us; we take the initiative toward others. This is simple teaching with endless applications.

The Lord God always makes the first move.

> For thus says the Lord GOD: Behold, I, I myself will search for my sheep and will seek them out. (Ezek. 34:11)

This section of Ezekiel is about God's people who have both left their true Shepherd and been abused by their leaders. Though the sheep show no inkling of turning back to the Lord, he seeks the lost, brings back the strays, and binds up the injured (vv. 11–24). His mercy and compassion lead the way.

The story has so many variations. Think of Hosea's persistent but quiet and even anonymous pursuit and care for his wayward wife. He did this as a way to illustrate God's relentless love. Think of Jesus and how he took the least-traveled route to get to one outcast Samaritan woman (John 4). Remember when he talked about his pursuit of that one lost sheep (Luke 15:4–6). He takes the initiative, especially toward those in need, even if it is just one.

Kings *receive* people. They consent to give you a five-minute audience, then off you go. Kings do not show up at your home or go out of their way to help you. But everything changes when King Jesus comes. This King leaves the palace precincts and finds you.

Jesus Pursues Us, We Pursue Each Other

All the biblical stories of the Lord moving toward people are stories of grace. Grace is God's moving toward us in Christ. He pursued us not because we called out so well and took the first step of self-reformation. We were simply sick and needed him. Or worse, we were enemies who were not inclined to surrender.[2]

He says "I love you" first, even when we respond with an indifferent shrug or the equivalent of a passing, "Oh, thanks." And in this we discover why it might be hard for us to move toward others: the one taking the initiative in the relationship—the one who loves most—is the one who risks humiliation.

But imagine this. You believe that Jesus pursues you. You are letting go of old lies that suggest he doesn't care and that you are forgotten. Because of Jesus, you no longer look for the easiest person to talk to when people gather. Instead, you move toward the quieter ones, the new person, and the outliers. Imagine a group of people who move toward each other—active more than passive, loving more than fearing rejection. They look glorious; they attract the world. This is an example of what the apostle Paul calls *putting on Christ* and is evidence of the Spirit of Christ at work in us.[3]

As you envision how to grow in moving toward others, think of those who have known hardships in their lives. For example, a man once shared with a small group that his past year had been the most difficult of his life. In response, no one said a word. No one ever approached him. No one asked, "Please, tell me more. How are you now? How can I pray for you?" Not one. It is no surprise that he kept to himself for the next ten years.

Too often we are silent when we know of someone's trouble. Silence is the same as turning away.

Jesus Listens, We Listen

So we move toward others. The extroverts among us seem to make it look easy. The more shy might be intimidated by the potential awkwardness or silence. But loving pursuit is neither easy nor natural to anyone. All of us need both humility and help from Scripture in order to navigate the early stages of a helpful conversation. Those initial steps might look like this:

- The Lord calls us family, so we greet warmly.
- The Lord knows our name, so we learn someone's name.
- The Lord knows seemingly irrelevant details about us, such as the number of hairs on our heads, so we take an interest in details. Is the person new to your gathering? Where does he or she live? Who does she live with? Does she work, go to school, manage a home?

What we hear might surprise us. After all, most people are not often asked about themselves, so we might hear much more than basic information. We might hear about events worth celebrating; we might hear of personal hardships.

The good and pleasant events might be a job completed well or a new relationship. But they also include a deeper good such as when we see something of the character of God in another—in the way he or she loves family and friends, serves, cares, or perseveres in trouble.

And there will be nonstop trouble, such as personal health struggles and those of family and friends, injustices at work, or broken relationships.

In response, we *listen*. This means we are undistracted, engaged, and affected by what they say. We share, in some small way, the delights of the good things and the burdens of the hard things. The script for eliciting these important matters can get fuzzy, and there will be more on that next, but we know this: there is always more to know.

> The purpose in a man's heart is like deep water,
> but a man of understanding will draw it out.
> (Prov. 20:5)

We hope to be that person of understanding. This can happen only if we pursue others as we have been pursued by Jesus.

Discussion and Response

1. Have you ever been pursued by someone who took a genuine interest in your life? How did that person do it? How was it encouraging to you?

2. We hope to be motivated by how Jesus has treated us. How would you say that Jesus has pursued you?

3. Why might you be reluctant to move toward others?

4. How do you hope to make the first move today and this week?

Lesson 3

Know the Heart

Know the heart, know the person. Our interest in helping one another pushes us beyond routine conversations and into the realm of the heart. A clear guide to this terrain can enrich all our relationships.

Someone asks, "How are you?"

You respond, "Fine, thank you. How are you?"

It is a pleasant greeting.

But when someone asks, "How are you?" and then stops everything and takes a seat to listen, you are inclined to say more.

Events and Circumstances of Life

At first, *more* might be a simple diary of the day's events.

A parent asks a twelve-year-old daughter, "How was your day at school?"

"Okay."

"Tell me a little about it."

"I had math, then history, then lunch."

This is a start, but we don't want our conversations to cover *only* events. We have a sense that there is something deeper. We want to know what is important to the other person, and this takes us into what Scripture calls the *heart.*[4]

Matters of the Heart

The heart can be veiled and difficult to know. We prefer to hide its less attractive thoughts and some of its hurts. But when we are willing to be a little more vulnerable, and others handle our hearts with care, we discover that knowing and being known are part of our design. These conversations are a pleasure, and they are essential if we are to care for, help, and encourage each other well.

Think of the heart as having layers and depth. It is compared to the roots of a tree (Jer. 17:5–8), waters that run deep (Prov. 20:5), and a treasure for which we must search (Matt. 6:20). Since it is quite busy, there is always more to discover, though sometimes it will take time, and trust, to draw it out.

Natural Desires

You know you have entered into the heart when you discover wants, affections, or desires. Here we store those things that are most important to us.

> We want rest and health for our bodies,
> the best for friends and family,
> protection from enemies,

work that is meaningful,
lives that contribute,
peace,
love.

These desires of the heart are important to the Lord, and he invites us to pour out our hearts to him (Ps. 62:8). That's how his love works. He shares in the pleasures and pains of his beloved. The Lord *hears* us in the fullest sense. He hears and is moved. He invites us to speak and responds with compassion, reminders of past faithfulness, and the certainty of his promises.

Then, as our response to him, we do this with each other. We invite others to speak. We enter into someone's world. We listen for those matters that are most important to the other person. We listen and track the person's emotions because that is where we find wants and desires.

"What have been the highlights of your day?"
"What has been especially hard?"

Questions like these set us in the right direction. They lead us to natural desires satisfied or denied, and they are typically the first step into the heart.

Moral Desires

Just beneath our swirling desires is the moral direction of our lives:

The good person out of the good treasure of his heart produces good, and the evil person out of his evil treasure produces evil, for out of the abundance of the heart his mouth speaks. (Luke 6:45)

A friend asked me, "How is your heart?"

Notice how he was reaching further in. He was especially interested in how my desires set a moral or spiritual course for my life.

Here we find that our hearts can be upright, steadfast, clean, penitent, and pure, or duplicitous, corrupt, hard, and overflowing with follies.

In other words, this man was essentially asking, "How are you doing in your spiritual battles? How are you handling life's temptations?" We usually give access to these places only in more seasoned relationships marked by love.

Godward Desires

Our moral direction is founded, of course, on a person. The direction of our hearts is never about mere law keeping or law breaking. In our hearts we know our Creator God (Rom. 1:19–21; 2:14–15), and all our life is in relation to him:

> When we violate his law, we dishonor his name and are turned away.
> When we love others, we honor him and love him.
> When we are afraid, we need to know him and his nearness more deeply.
> When angry, we turn from him and live for our own desires above all.
> When ashamed, we turn from him because we believe the lie that he has turned away from us.

We all live before the face of God, whether we are consciously aware of that or not. Life is intensely personal. He pursues us and invites us to know him through Jesus—that is what is on *his* heart. We, in turn, respond in one of two ways. Either our godly desire is aroused and we want to hear, know Jesus, come to him, join him in his kingdom work, and speak with him. Or our selfish desire attaches to other gods and kingdoms that we think are more valuable. To put it another way, we trust in him or we trust in ourselves and the objects of our affection. We turn either toward him or away from him.

In the very depths of our heart, it is not so much *what* we love but *who* we love.[5]

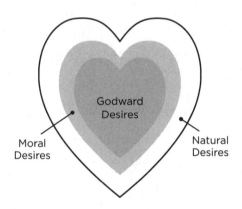

Know and Enjoy

Here is how we move more deeply into someone's life:

1. Ask, "How are you?" Then follow the strong emotions. This is the way into the heart, and this is where

help begins. We listen for the joys and sorrows, the hopes and fears, and we take an interest in them.

2. Enjoy the good. We search for "love, joy, peace, patience, kindness, goodness, faithfulness, gentleness, [and] self-control" (Gal. 5:22–23) and other character qualities that look like Jesus. When we see or hear those reflections of Christ, we enjoy them, point them out, and simply *like* the person.

3. Have compassion when there is trouble, and there will be a lot (John 16:33). The longer you walk with someone, the more trouble you will hear. We want to grow in compassion when we hear it.

4. As you continue to walk together, you might discover a spiritual foundation that is a composite of faith in Jesus and trust in self. Here especially we talk about Jesus and his love, and we pray that we would know him better. When we turn away, we have forgotten who he is, and the prescription is to know him better.

We are all saints, sufferers, and sinners who hope to be more transparent with each other. You too will be open about your affections when someone asks. We want to know others and also be known by them.

Discussion and Response

1. Below is a useful diagram. At the very center is the heart. The circle around the heart represents the body. Together they comprise the actual person. As you move out from the center, the other concentric circles are examples of the shaping influences on our lives. The inner circle includes those influences we can see, the outer circle contains those

that are less visible. The arrow suggests that there is constant engagement between our hearts and the living God, back and forth. The arrow also suggests that our hearts are *affected* by all the circumstances of life (the arrow comes *at* us) and *interpret* all of life (the arrow goes *out* from us). We are, indeed, very busy.

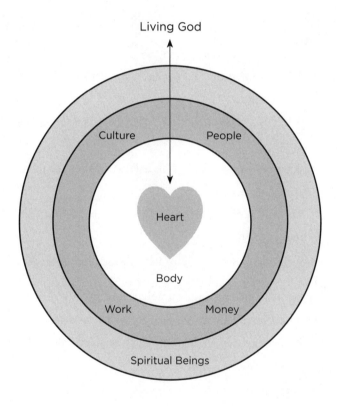

How does this self-understanding make sense of your own soul?

What questions do you have?

2. What questions help you make your way into your own heart?

- What do you love? This asks about the objects of your desire.
- What makes you happy? This listens for desires satisfied.
- What makes you sad? This asks about desires postponed or denied.
- What makes you angry? This too asks about desires denied.
- What do you fear? This asks about desires at risk.

We want to practice on ourselves and grow in transparency before the Lord. As we grow in understanding of how our heart works, we can learn to move more deeply into someone else's life.

3. Practice seeing the good—not just good circumstances but moral goodness. Notice when the person is patient when treated badly, kind when treated unkindly, forgiving, gentle, and able to say no to renegade desires. As a general rule, you hope to see this before you talk about more difficult matters.

- In the last few days, what good things have you seen in other people?

- Why is seeing the good important?

Lesson 4

Know the Critical Influences

If we are to help wisely, we want to know the heart *and* the significant influences on the heart. Among those many influences are two representatives in particular: other people and our physical bodies.

Our hearts are always up to something. As we might expect, there is unceasing activity around those things that are important to us. We love, fret, plan, rest, avoid, worship, hide, and much more. Meanwhile, the world around us is also tireless and active. We lose jobs, spouses are angry with us, and cars break down. We are invited for a meal, we recover from sickness, and we are loved. Life always comes at us with hard things and good things. If we are to know and help each other, we will reside close to where someone's world and heart meet.

Notice in the diagram that the arrow moves back and forth between all those things outside of us and our hearts. Our bodies, our work, our wealth, our culture, other people, and even spiritual forces are all in engaged in negotiations with our hearts, either challenging our beliefs or confirming them. God, of course, is over and through them all, and it is his voice we want to hear most clearly.

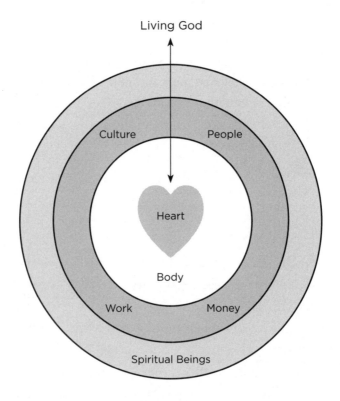

The sheer number of influences on the heart is impossible to fully know. Our goal is to identify those influences that have been most important. Among those that consistently top the list are the impact of other people and the effects of body and brain weakness.

People Heal, People Harm

People have the most obvious impact on our lives. We can be dirt poor, but we judge life by our relationships. When we are rich with close friends and family, life is good. When isolated and detached, no amount of money can counterbalance such hardships. When rejected or abused, the aftershocks seem to never end. Our relationships bless, and they curse.

Psalm 133 extols the blessing of unity.

> Behold, how good and pleasant it is
>   when brothers dwell in unity!
> It is like the precious oil on the head,
>   running down on the beard,
> on the beard of Aaron,
>   running down on the collar of his robes!
>   (vv. 1–2)

Meanwhile, the majority of the psalms identify the pain of isolation, friends who act like enemies, enemies who act like enemies, and the toll of injustice.

We know this: God is active in the midst of hard relationships, victimization, and oppression. The Israelites' exodus from Egypt began because God was responding to the cries of slaves, even though they were not even crying out to him. Jesus himself, our Great High Priest, entered into this world of being misunderstood and violated as he was "made like his brothers in every respect, so that he might become a merciful and faithful high priest" who acts on behalf of the hurt and mistreated (Heb. 2:17).

Yet while God is active, so is Satan. We know that Satan uses such difficulties to raise questions about God's care and compassion. Does God really care? Would a good father let his children go through such things? All painful circumstances can incite a confusing din of competing voices that reveal or overwhelm our hearts, and we can have competing responses:

- We can trust in God's power and justice and remain thankful.
- We can become embittered and take matters into our own hands.
- We can remain confident in God's love because we have our eyes fixed on Jesus.
- We can believe that God is distant and indifferent to our pain.

Helpers walk carefully here. These responses reveal important matters, but when we care for others, we rarely rush into the heart's responses first. Instead, we linger on the relationships that have been painful. We wouldn't begin a conversation with Job by saying, "How have you, before the Lord, responded to your children's deaths and your own aches and pains?" Those questions bypass compassion and are often unnecessary.

This does not mean that we postpone speaking about the Lord, but only that we walk with care toward another person's heart. Help, at its best, brings Christ early and often. When we hear of overwhelming circumstances and relationships, we want to help one another speak these troubles to the Lord, ask for his compassion and strength, and be assured of his faithful love.

When we hear about someone's good relationships, we are blessed along with them. When we hear about hard relationships, we take notice, hope at some time to hear more, and ask how we can pray.

Our Bodies Are Strong, Our Bodies Are Weak

The impact of other people is rivaled by the impact of our bodies. Our bodies *are* us, but they also act as a kind of influence on our hearts similar to the way that people do. So, in the diagram, the body is represented as a circle, which suggests that, while it *is* us, it also affects us. Poor health, for example, is perceived as something that *happens* to us, and it is among the most important of circumstances that happen to us.

"How is your health?" This is the most common greeting throughout the world.

"Could you pray for healing?" This is our most common prayer request.

We are physical beings and always will be. The time is coming when our bodies will be renewed, but for now, they can be finicky. At their best our bodies—and our brains—are strong and healthy. Everything seems to work well, and there are no aches or pains that demand our attention. Otherwise, our bodies are weak and wasting away, in which case they can become preoccupations and intrusions into the work of daily life. The apostle Paul summarizes it this way:

> Though our outer self [our body] is wasting away, our inner self [our heart or our soul] is being renewed day by day. (2 Cor. 4:16)

Our aim is to have a growing awareness of these physical strengths and weaknesses.

We all understand something about the body's weaknesses. We know about poor vision, chronic pain, strokes, and broken bones. Yet like all our knowledge of each other, we want to know more. For example, consider how we bring order to life. Some people can identify clear steps for accomplishing a particular goal; others are more haphazard. This process occurs through physical—that is, brain-related—strengths or weaknesses. Some people bring intense focus to detail; others see the big picture and forget the specifics. These too can be a result of brain differences.

Recent study into the connection between the brain and behavior has given more insight into challenging problems such as dementing adults and the learning differences of children. Recent advances in modern psychiatry have alerted us to the interdependence of our thinking, emotions, and brain functioning. We don't have to be experts in these areas of study, but we do want to learn as we can, receive help from those with more experience, and be humble in the face of human complexity.

When we hear of good health, we enjoy that person's blessings; when we hear of disability and sickness, we hope to understand more, have compassion, and pray.

- We give thanks for good health.
- We pray for healing during sickness.
- We pray for faith to be renewed during sickness.

Here is a general rule: the more you understand a person's physical weaknesses, the more patient you will be with that person.

The Power of Circumstances

The circumstances of life do not have the power to turn us away from Jesus or to make us love him more—those are the jurisdiction of the heart. But they *can* make life easier or more miserable, and they can be difficult tests that reveal surprising things about what was once quiet in our hearts. When we run into a detour at the worst time, we notice that our hearts are more angry and demanding than we had thought.

So we listen at the intersection of life and the heart. There we find that those people who seemed so stern or distant have been hurt, and their kindness is apparent with only a little digging; or we might find that the fearful may be the spiritual giants among us, and the violated who speak openly are among our most brave. There are endless depths and recesses within any person. We have the privilege of sharing and knowing some of these places. Though we can never know each other exhaustively, we can know each other accurately and truly.

Discussion and Response

1. Endless influences shape our lives: people, bodies and brains, education, climate, local culture, political leaders, race, and wars. What has been the prominent influence on your life? How has it affected your heart?

2. Our era has been more careful in describing brain-related differences. Which ones have been helpful for how you have understood yourself or others? How has knowing the particulars about someone's physical weaknesses contributed to your patience and love for that person?

3. Psalm 130 is an example of how we can move naturally from circumstances to the heart:

   Out of the depths I cry to you, O LORD!
       O Lord, hear my voice!
   Let your ears be attentive
       to the voice of my pleas for mercy!

   If you, O LORD, should mark iniquities,
       O Lord, who could stand?

But with you there is forgiveness,
>   that you may be feared. (vv. 1–4)

Whatever the psalmist's circumstances, they are extreme. The psalmist describes an experience that could not be closer to death while still having life. But he directs his pleas to the Lord. He remembers this: if the Lord, in his loving-kindness, forgives his enemies, then we can be assured that he will be with us during our time of need.

We do not deny the hardships of life. Rather, we want to speak them to the God who hears, remember his promises and faithful love, and grow in trusting him.

Take time to pray that we would be able to speak similar psalms.

Lesson 5

Be Personal and Pray

Though we might think that real help comes through dramatic and new insights, most help tends to come in more ordinary ways. It comes through our personal engagement with each other, our attention to Christ, and prayer.

On the next page, once again is the diagram of the heart that is embedded in innumerable circles.

It is a simple structure, yet it gives us leads on every human struggle. It provides a way to interpret all psychiatric or psychological problems, which are often significantly influenced by the body and the brain. It also explains why we feel most whole during a time of church worship, singing hymns and praises—it extends to the farthest reaches of our souls or hearts.[6]

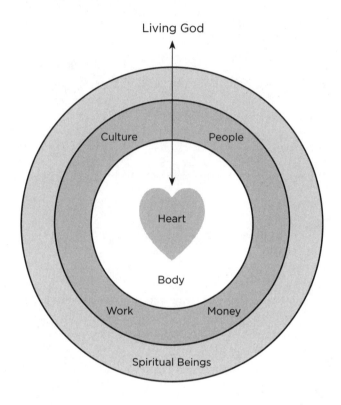

Keep in mind that Jesus Christ is not merely for our spiritual lives, as if *spiritual* were distinct from our thinking, emotions, or relationships. Instead, all of life is spiritual, in that Christ is our comfort, our forgiveness, our honor, our justice, our power, our joy, and our hope. Our very structure makes the knowledge of Jesus and our trust in him the center of the human heart, and only when we rest in Jesus can we truly flourish as his people.

Equipped with these rudiments, we want to draw out more and more applications that guide us in wise, helpful conversations.

Be personal and pray—those are two skills we hope to master.

Be Personal

Here is something true and rich: God is personal, so we are personal with him and each other.

Personal means that God comes close to his people. When he comes close, he speaks to us and invites us to respond, and when we respond to him, he hears. This means that he listens and is actually influenced by what we say. We could think of it as being invited into his home, where he speaks openly and with love, and he offers the best of divine hospitality. All that is almost too much to take in, but then he invites us to speak of what is important to us, and as we speak, he is engaged, undistracted, and responsive.

We could call it fellowship, even communion.

The life of Jesus on earth is evidence of God's personal fellowship with us. He spoke and listened and was moved by what he saw and heard. Every mention of his compassion and mercy is evidence that he is the personal God. Think back to his conversation with the Samaritan woman again (John 4:1–42). He pursued this outcast woman, engaged in the longest recorded conversation in the New Testament, and revealed himself to her as the Christ. He came close to her as servant, friend, and God.

Our help, in response, is personal. We are a composite of servant and friend who, as servant, places a priority on the interests of others, and, as friend, enters in, enjoys the person, bears burdens, and even shares what is on our own hearts.

We enjoy others and the good things they have received:

"I am so happy for you."

"Let's celebrate together."

"What a great gift. This is just wonderful."

We also enjoy them and the good things that come out of their hearts:

"Your openness about your life has been such a lesson to me about grace."

"Thank you so much for your concern for me. It reminds me that I am not alone."

"I so appreciate seeing the patience and kindness you give to your children."

We have compassion as we share in their burdens and sufferings:

"I'm so sorry."

"This seems so hard. Could you tell me a little more?"

"You are on my heart."

We "rejoice with those who rejoice, [and] weep with those who weep" (Rom. 12:15) because doing so reflects the character of God.

The rule for being personal is to say *something* when you are given access to someone's treasures. It doesn't have to be much. What guides our responses is both the Golden Rule (Matt. 7:12[7]) and humility. The Golden Rule asks, "What have other people said *to me* that was helpful and encouraging?" Humility asks, "What could help and encourage *you*?" When we don't know what to say, we ask for help.

As a variation of the Golden Rule you could also consider what has been *unhelpful* to you and others. For example, it is almost always unhelpful to give advice to someone who is troubled unless the troubled one asks. Advice is what *we* would do in another's situation, even though we might never have been in that situation. It typically sounds teacher-like, and it bypasses compassion. It is rarely personal. So hold back your advice unless it is requested.

Talking about *yourself* might also be unhelpful, at least initially:

"Really? My mom had Alzheimer's disease too."

"I get depressed sometimes too. Last year I was so worn out from . . ."

Your intent might be to further invite the person to be open, and in some relationships these comments might actually do that. But they can also change the topic from what is on the other person's heart to what was on your own. So if you do offer your own analogous story, be sure to get back to what is happening with the other person.

Pray

One certain way to be personal is to pray. That is evidence that someone is on our hearts. Prayer joins together our knowledge of others, our love for them, and our knowledge of God and his promises.

It might go like this: you move toward a new person after church. You greet her and ask about her. In response you get a few facts—where she works, where she lives, how long she has lived there. She mentions that she is between jobs.

During the next week you pray for her a couple of times. The next time you see her, you ask her about her job search. When she says that it is stalled, you ask a little more—what work she has done, what work she would like to do. Then you pray:

"This seems pretty hard. How can I pray for you?"
"You could pray that I would be able to find work soon."
"Could I pray for you now?"

You are going further into the heart and matters of importance to her. Other questions follow:

"Any new ideas for work?"

You might ask a few broader questions:

"Where did you go to church before?"

Meanwhile, you are always listening for what is most important. You are listening for her affections, her emotions.

As you read Scripture you notice passages that can guide how you pray for her. You tell her about these passages and ask if there are others that are important to her. You invite her to a small group in which others can know her and she, them.

Here are the essentials of help and care:

Be personal—that is, move toward people, know others, be moved by those things that are important.

Pray for and with people—the best care identifies the needs in our lives that can be met only in Jesus Christ. Those are our most important and deepest needs.

Once invited into another person's life, there are so many questions and troubles to consider:

"What do I do with my angry daughter?"
"My husband hit me this week. What should I do?"
"I feel like a failure in everything."

You don't have to know all the answers. Humility and love want to know more, so you ask for more. You ask what has been helpful and unhelpful. You consider how to pray. Then there is always more help available in the larger body of Christ, so we seek help together.

Discussion and Response

1. When have you been blessed by the personal responses of others? In other words, when has someone encouraged you by really listening to and hearing you?

2. One of the shocking revelations of the character of God occurs when, in response to the wavering affections of Israel, the Lord says:

> My heart recoils within me;
>> my compassion grows warm and tender.
>>> (Hos. 11:8)

"Recoils" is not the same as *withdraws*. It is more that God's heart is strongly moved and aroused on behalf of his people. God is moved by his people; we too want to be moved by the pleasures and hardships of those we love. As we think about the fact that God is moved by us, we hope to be even more responsive to others. How might these realities affect how you pray?

3. The movement from knowing others to praying with them face-to-face can be hard. Why might that be? How do you hope to grow in praying with others?

4. Take some time to pray with each other.

Lesson 6

Talk about Suffering

Hardships and suffering are everywhere, and Scripture counters by speaking to our troubles on nearly every page. The exodus story leads the way.

Since so many of our conversations are about hardships, we want to know more about what God says to those who suffer. Most of us have thought about these things. We all have some ideas of what God says. Our interest is to refine what we know and add to it.

Where do we begin?

Some of our struggles are clearly identified in Scripture. For example, we can look up "fear" or "anxiety" in a Bible concordance, and hundreds of passages are immediately available. But what do we do when Scripture does not clearly identify a particular problem? It seems relatively quiet with regard to the growing number of psychiatric diagnoses, which are pressing matters for so many. In response, we ask for help from other wise people, and we keep listening to those who struggle. As we do, we notice two things:

1. Hardships are unique. No two forms of suffering are identical.

2. Hardships share something in common. They are painful and can leave us feeling at the end of ourselves. This is the reason why one psalm can speak to so many different troubles.

Here is one of those stories that extends to so much human misery. It does not identify all the possible assaults we could experience, but it does provide a master story to guide us.

The Wilderness Story

The exodus narrative began with God's compassion and deliverance: "The people of Israel groaned because of their slavery and cried out for help. Their cry for rescue from slavery came up to God. And God heard their groaning" (Ex. 2:23–24). The Lord then showed his mighty power over Egypt, and he led them out. The plan was to move through the wilderness and to the Promised Land, but the wilderness journey became longer and more difficult than anyone anticipated.

The wilderness is hard, and we respond with compassion.

The wilderness is, indeed, a place of destitution and powerlessness. If you have ever felt that way during your troubles, this is your story. The wilderness feels as though all is lost and you can't take another step. Threats are everywhere. As people who want to help, the wilderness journeys of those we love will evoke our compassion. We grieve with those who grieve, we move closer to them, and we pray that they would be strengthened.

More is happening in the wilderness than hardships.

Things are not exactly what they seem. Though our senses tell us that we are alone, the Lord is there, and since he is the source of life, life will come even in an otherwise lifeless land. This desert is where water comes from rocks and manna appears every morning.

It is also where the Lord tests and trains his royal children so they can see what is actually in their hearts and can ascend with maturity and wisdom to the royal courts (Deut. 8:1–3; James 1:2–5). The test goes to the depths of our souls: will we believe and trust him when our circumstances seem dire?

In the original wilderness testing, the people forgot God; they complained against him, which is a way of holding him in contempt; they pined away for Egypt; and they looked for help apart from the Lord. So often we replicate their journey, and when life is hard we trust what our senses tell us more than what God says.

In response to our wavering allegiances, Jesus himself entered the wilderness. It turns out that the wilderness journey, which is the path along which God takes his royal children, is the way of King Jesus (Matt. 4:1–11). After humanity's many failures in the wilderness, our champion took over where we had failed. But his path was different. Whereas Israel had manna, Jesus would be sustained only by the words of his Father, rather than bread. Whereas Satan was in the shadows during the exodus journey, he would personally take up the fight and focus his spiritual weaponry on the weakened Messiah. His strategies, though, were familiar: "God's ways are not good. Trust in yourself, trust in me, trust in dead idols." When trouble comes, we can be certain that we will hear Satan's lies that raise doubts of the Lord's generosity, love, and truthfulness.

Our King voluntarily went into this most arduous place where he believed and recited the words of his Father. Those words were his food and satisfaction. They were all he needed to be strengthened and successful, and his success would change everything.

In other words, in our own wilderness our aspiration is to have eyes to see Jesus.

The wilderness is an opportunity for faith.

Now we enter into the wilderness story knowing that Jesus has already been victorious and has given us the Spirit to do what we could not do before. We can turn to the Lord rather than away from him during intense troubles.

This new story is for us all—those who are familiar with PTSD, trauma, victimization and abuse, loss, and fear. It is also the seminal story for temptation, so it is foundational for all addiction. Our task is to inhabit it and make it our own.

Notice what happens when the exodus becomes *our* story. It begins with *our* deliverance from slavery. "I am the LORD your God, who brought you out of the land of Egypt, out of the house of slavery" (Ex. 20:2). God has somehow heard our groaning, even though we were not yet calling out to him. He demonstrated his power over Satan, and he determined that we would belong to him.

Since our King was led into destitute places, we can be sure that we too, who follow the King, will be taken into hardships. In the back of our minds we think that good fathers should shield us from hardship. We might get a skinned knee and believe he still loves us. But what father would let his child go through shameful abuse? This question is hard to answer, but we know this: the Father loved his perfect Son, who went through the worst of suffering and shame, so he certainly loves us who are joined to his Son by faith. The Father also can be trusted to be the righteous Judge who will make things right. This confidence sustained Jesus through his humiliation: "When he was reviled, he did not revile in return; when he suffered, he did not threaten, but continued entrusting himself to him who judges justly" (1 Pet. 2:23). We can share in his confidence.

Hardships will come.
Jesus has gone before us in hardships and knows us.
The love of the Father pursues us in our hardships.
The Father's justice, which will silence all perpetrators and restore his people, is assured.

Jesus is with us now by his Spirit, and he prepares a place for us in the land promised. Having defeated Satan, forgiven our sins, and successfully gone through the wilderness on our behalf, he guides us through the wilderness to our home with him. As we persevere by trusting him, he strengthens us in our weakness. In this we bring honor to his name.

Cry Out to the Lord

The first and most important way to express this trust—or strength in weakness—is simply to speak to him:

> Out of the depths I cry to you, O LORD!
> > O Lord, hear my voice!
> Let your ears be attentive
> > to the voice of my pleas for mercy! (Ps. 130:1–2)

This is among the easiest and hardest things to do. Children can do it, but it demands that sophisticated combination of both human neediness and personal confidence in Jesus. It can feel quite unnatural at first. It can feel like baby talk. But it is much more than that, because it is the Spirit of God who gives us words to speak. Those words are honest, open, filled with questions, and they hold on, sometimes barely, to Jesus Christ and what he has done.

Scripture—God's personal communication to us—speaks to us in our misery. Though it might not identify the precise nature of our wilderness, once we identify our specific struggles as *suffering*, God's Word says a lot.

Discussion and Response

1. Have any particular Scripture passages about suffering become especially meaningful to you?

2. Can you connect the wilderness story to modern problems such as depression, other problems that might be treated with medication, or struggles that have been hard to find in Scripture? The wilderness story encompasses all types of hardships, including those that come from irregularities in the brain or the body. Among the strengths of this narrative is that we don't have to know the precise cause of the trouble to inhabit it, and it accepts all kinds of trouble.

3. How would you pray for someone, using the wilderness story? Here are some of the spiritual realities gleaned from the exodus master story that can guide you:[8]

   • Life is hard. The Son suffered, and those who follow the Son will suffer (1 Pet. 4:12).
   • Speak honestly and often to the Lord. This is critical. Just speak, groan, have someone read you a psalm, and say a weak "Amen."
   • Expect to get to know God better while in this wilderness (Phil. 3:10–11).
   • All eyes on Jesus. Keep an eye out in Scripture for the Suffering Servant. He has entered into your suffering, and you can enter into his. (Isaiah 39–53; John 10–21).
   • Live by faith; see the unseen (Heb. 11:1). Normal eyesight is not enough. Your eyes will tell you that

God is far away and silent. The truth is that he is close—invisible, but close. He has a unique affection for fellow sufferers. So get help to build up your spiritual vision. Search Scripture. Enlist others to help, to pray, to remind you of the truth. Ask the God of comfort to comfort you.

- God is God (Job 38–42); we are his children who do not understand the details of his ways (Psalm 131; Isa. 55:8). Humility before the King can quiet some of your questions.
- Get help. Talk to those who have suffered; read their books; listen to them. You are not alone.
- Confess sin. This doesn't mean that sin is necessarily the cause of suffering. It simply means that suffering tests our loyalties, and our loyalties might be exposed as being more divided than we knew (James 1:2–4). Also, confession is a regular feature of daily life. It helps you to see the cross of Jesus more clearly and is the quickest way to see the persistent and lavish love of God (Heb. 12:1–12).
- Look ahead. We need spiritual vision for what is happening now and for where the universe is heading. We are on a pilgrimage that ends at the temple of God (Pss. 23:6; 84:1–4).

All these spiritual realities are not intended to give us answers to everyone's questions. Both our own suffering and the suffering of others compel us to humility, in which we aspire to be more like children than teachers. These do, however, remind us that God speaks about our suffering and to sufferers.

Lesson 7

Talk about Sin

Wise conversations will talk about sin. Though we might prefer to avoid this, we know that we all struggle with sin, and we all need each other's help. As with suffering, we offer that help very carefully.

We usually listen for pleasures and pains first. Once there, we often witness a quiet but persistent endurance of faith in Jesus. When we see this, we are blessed by it and consider ways to encourage the person in it. But we also might witness doubts, struggles of faith, and sin.

The hard circumstances of life *feel* like our most pressing problem. Our struggles with faith and following Christ in obedience are even more important. Suffering, for example, cannot separate us from the Lord, but hard hearts and persistent sin break our relationship with God.

They will eventually separate us from others, and, if left unattended, end with misery that far outweighs our present hardships.

Since we are saints who sin, how can we talk about sin to those who might be caught in it?

See the Good

Keep this general rule in mind: we talk about the hard things and good things before we talk about the bad. For example, the apostle Paul wrote about serious sins to the church in Corinth. Yet he starts with the good:

> I give thanks to my God always for you because of the grace of God that was given you in Christ Jesus, that in every way you were enriched in him in all speech and all knowledge—even as the testimony about Christ was confirmed among you—so that you are not lacking in any gift. (1 Cor. 1:4–7)

In this, Paul takes his cue from how his life is tucked into Jesus, and the Father identifies him as a saint first. We want to do the same.

We All Sin

But we are saints who sin. The era in which we live—on the far side of Christ's sacrifice for sins and his sending of the Spirit to us—is not sin-free. It is condemnation-free and full of forgiveness, and it is an era when we are no longer slaves to sin and are liberated and empowered to fight against it. But it is not sin-free. We can still organize our worlds around our own selfish desires; we can believe what we feel more than what God has said and done in Jesus Christ; and we can discount his holiness, beauty, and power.

So we talk about sin "with all humility and gentleness, with patience, bearing with one another in love" (Eph. 4:2). We talk about our own sin and the sin of those we want to help, and we would like these conversations to be good. Not that sin itself is good, but we are actually blessed when we can *see* our sin.

When we see our sin, we are more grateful for forgiveness of sins because we understand that we have been forgiven for much, whereas "he who is forgiven little, loves little" (Luke 7:47).

When we see sin, we are close to the light. Only when we *don't* see our sin should we be suspicious of our hearts.

> If we say we have no sin, we deceive ourselves, and
> the truth is not in us. (1 John 1:8)

Our goal is to contribute to a community in which it is increasingly natural to talk about sin and ask each other for help.

Ways to Talk about Sin

Sin becomes public in three different ways: someone confesses it, we see it, or we are told about it. Each of these suggests different responses. For example, a person who confesses is already in the battle against sin. But a person who is found out might not have entered the battle yet.

You will adjust your engagement according to the other person's honesty and self-awareness.

Following are some ways to enter into the discussion.

Say Something

The first words are the hardest. When you have no idea what to say, be honest:

> "You have been on my heart. I have really appreciated your willingness to say that you struggle with porn, but I have been concerned that people might leave you alone. Could we talk about it?"

> "Something you said the other day has really stuck with me. It was when you got angry at your wife. Could we talk about it?"

> "I know you have been really busy with work and traveling more than usual. It got me thinking about how my own struggle with temptations can be more severe when there are fewer people around who know me. How have you been dealing with your temptations when you are on the road?"

If you have clear evidence of sinful actions, be specific. If you have concerns or questions, simply raise them without accusing. All this can be hard, but, if we are left with regrets, most of us regret *not* saying something.

"We" More Than "You"

A turning point in a man's fight with illegal drugs occurred when his wife discovered that he was using again, and she responded, "What are *we* going to do?" In other words, "How will we fight this together?" In response to her husband's sin, she moved closer. This began a process that included a clear plan, years of sobriety, and a growing relationship.

"We are in this together." That might mean you don't fully understand the nature of another's sin, but you will be right next to him, with patience and kindness, in the battle. It can also mean that you *do* understand his sin because you too struggle with a variant of it. Whatever sin you see in others, a brief search usually reveals that you too are vulnerable to the same kind of sin. Your version might look different but comes from the same renegade desires.

Questions More Than Exhortations

As Jesus speaks with people who are caught in sin, he often asks questions. "Why are you thinking these things?" "Which is lawful on the Sabbath, to do good or evil?" (e.g., Mark 3:4). "How can the guests of the bridegroom fast while the bridegroom is with them?" (e.g., Luke 5:34). These questions often weave together two purposes. First, Jesus is inviting us to think about something. Sin tends to look less attractive when it is closely inspected. Second, Jesus is inviting us to a conversation. He is asking questions in order to get a response. "Come now, let us reason together" is a standard way the Lord approaches our sin.

Among the questions we might ask is, "How can I help?"

Sin Is Personal

Sin is always about God, whether we are aware of that or not. It is bent on independence. When we are angry, our anger is not *consciously* about God, but it is about God (James 4:1–4). Even our grumbling and complaining are about God. They say, "What have you done for me recently?" They hold God in contempt (Num. 14:11).

Clarity comes from knowing both our hearts and our Lord:

1. We know that our sin is first against God, and we confess it, as we would in any relationship.
2. We know that our Lord is quick to forgive.
3. We set out to know Jesus better. We must not have known and loved him as we thought we did. Perhaps we have thought that the Lord is a policeman looking for the slightest infraction, and we, in turn, have been looking for ways to get out from under the burden of one law after another. So we counter any resident myths with the accurate knowledge of Jesus, who loved us while we were his enemies, and we set out to enjoy both him and his divine hospitality. Anything else will end in meaninglessness, misery, and other forays into sin.

End Confession with "Thank You"

The Lord's forgiveness might seem too good to be true. Our instinct is, after confession, to go into exile and reform ourselves so we will be acceptable to our Father.

But keep the story of the prodigal son in mind (Luke 15:11–24). Our Father is simply inclined to forgive. This distinguishes him from all invented gods and from all of humanity. He is eager to forgive at the slightest hint that we acknowledge our sin and guilt (Jer. 3:3).

Satan's lie suggests that God is like a mere human and his grace and love are restricted and stingy. May we never be fooled by such lies. We are a people who were loved even when we opposed the Lord, we rest in Jesus's completed sacrifice, we rely on the Spirit's presence and power, and we can have hints of joy in everyday life.

We could summarize the process this way: after confession, end with "thank you." When we say this, we have confronted both Satan's lies and our own sense that grace is for other people but not for us.

Could you imagine a community in which we can confess our sins to one another, and we respond to such confessions and pleas with humility, gentleness, patience, and prayer?

Discussion and Response

1. Has anyone ever spoken to you about your sin in a helpful way? How did she do that? Has anyone every spoken to you about your sin in a way that was unhelpful? Why was it unhelpful?

2. Here is a question for personal reflection rather than group discussion. One goal for all God's people is to be able to identify one area of sin and see how this sin is personal. Can you name one? Do you confess it? Do you end in thanks? Are you okay speaking about it publicly? Identifying our own sin keeps us turned toward the Life, and it promotes humility and patience as we speak with others. If there is secret sin, whom will you speak to about it?

3. We will not be speaking to others about their sin every day. We will speak about good things and hard things much more often. But if we love, there will be times when speaking about sin and temptations is the order of the day. Parents do this with their children. We hope to do it better with each other. Do you have concerns about this? Are there any particular ways that you hope to grow in it?

Lesson 8

Remember and Reflect

Caring for One Another has identified ordinary features of person-to-person engagement. There is nothing new here. The purpose
has been to remember and live out applications of the gospel of Jesus Christ. But in that,
the very power of God is further on display,
and the church is strengthened and drawn
together.

We have set out to do the "work of ministry" that is
essential to a fully functioning church, and we set out to
do it "with all humility and gentleness, with patience,
bearing with one another in love" (Eph. 4:2). We do
this work in small steps, being a little more alert in everyday conversations, a little more confident that the
Lord uses ordinary people. We are just moving toward
one person, then another, knowing, seeing good things,

bearing burdens, praying for and praying with. Who would have known that in all this, we have been contributing to the unity, protection, and growth of the church?

> [The Lord] gave the apostles, the prophets, the evangelists, the shepherds and teachers, to equip the saints for the work of ministry, for building up the body of Christ, until we all attain to the unity of the faith and of the knowledge of the Son of God, to mature manhood, to the measure of the stature of the fullness of Christ, so that we may no longer be children, tossed to and fro by the waves and carried about by every wind of doctrine, by human cunning, by craftiness in deceitful schemes. (Eph. 4:11–14)

For all this, we need power, and that is exactly what we have received, or we could say that is exactly *who* we have received. Since we have set out on a course that is "in him," both with Jesus and toward him, and life with Jesus is now lived out in and through his Spirit, we expect power that revives our souls—power in weakness, but power. This power is inevitable when we call out to him for help and love in his name. This power is on display when, through our mutual care, we gradually mature and become less prone to being "tossed to and fro" by the less-than-biblical chatter that always surrounds us.

These messages are everywhere. They typically attempt to undermine the extent of the Lord's love or our need for him:

"You aren't good enough. No wonder you are having so many hardships in your life. You'd better believe more. You have to work harder."

We counter this as we remember together the God who makes the first move toward us, who invites us to call out to him, and who loves not because we are so lovable but because he is love.

A second message is just as dangerous:

"You *are* good enough. Just believe in yourself. Jesus will give you the things you want."

In response, we remind each other that just as Israel needed manna every day, we need his forgiving and empowering grace—his very presence—every day. And the path we are on will not necessarily yield increased prestige before our neighbors or place us first in line for anything. Such a path would feed the pride and independence that we hope to see die. Rather, we follow Jesus, the crucified one, and we will have hardships. Yet, somehow, even in hardships we still taste the heavenly banquet that truly satisfies our souls.

Isn't it interesting that the maturity that makes us less susceptible to these myths comes about as we grow up into being God's children? As his children we pour out our hearts to our Father, and we stand on the firm foundation of Jesus, who is our peace, acceptance, and power. This takes us back to where we began. God uses ordinary people and their increasingly wise, childlike, God-dependent conversations to build his church. These do not depend on our brilliance in order to be helpful; they depend on Jesus, his strength, our weakness, and our humble response to him.

As we grow in this spiritual care for one another, we will indeed hear of human struggles that are more intense and more complicated than we thought possible, and we might feel like an inept child more than a dependent one. We will hear about matters of life and death. We will hear stories that might, at first, seem foreign to us. We certainly *hope* to hear of these, because we know these struggles are everywhere. When we do, we will be moved by what we hear, we will pray with and pray for, and *we will seek help*. Wisdom, humility, and love seek the help of those who have more experience than we do—pastors, friends who have gone through similar problems, friends who have helped those with similar problems, and professional helpers. This is the church working together.

It starts with small steps toward each other and life *with* each other.

Discussion and Response

1. What stands out in your own summary of these eight lessons?

2. What has been different in your conversations as a result of doing this study?

3. Humility seeks help. Can you imagine how a confusing conversation with another person could lead naturally to the two of you seeking more help? When would you do that?

4. What's next? What would help you to grow in these wise and helpful conversations? How do you aspire to grow as a child of God?

Notes

1. Augustine, *Letters 100–155,* vol. 2, *The Works of Saint Augustine: A Translation for the 21st Century* (Hyde Park, NY: New City Press, 2003), Letters 118, 116.
2. "If while we were enemies we were reconciled to God by the death of his Son, much more, now that we are reconciled, shall we be saved by his life" (Rom. 5:10).
3. See Rom. 13:12, 14; Gal. 3:27.
4. Since the heart is so important, Scripture has a rich vocabulary for it, such as *soul, mind, spirit,* and *inner parts.* Each word has a slightly different emphasis, but each identifies this center of our being.
5. Our hearts can, as a result, rejoice in the Lord, trust him, love him, and worship him, or turn away from the Lord, be stubborn and rebellious, prefer the world and lusts of the flesh, and worship idols.
6. This is a reminder that other words stand in for the heart.
7. "Whatever you wish that others would do to you, do also to them, for this is the Law and the Prophets."
8. Adapted from Ed Welch, "10 Things to Do During Suffering," CCEF website, March 25, 2014, accessed November 6, 2017, https://www.ccef.org/resources/blog/ten-things-do-during -suffering.

General Index

Scripture Index

Scripture Index

Restoring Christ to Counseling and Counseling to the Church

COUNSELING
ccef.org/counseling

WRITING
ccef.org/resources

TEACHING
ccef.org/courses

EVENTS
ccef.org/events

"CCEF is all about giving hope and help with a 'heart.' If you want to learn how to effectively use God's Word in counseling, this is your resource!"

Joni Eareckson Tada, Founder and CEO, Joni and Friends International Disability Center

"The vision of the centrality of God, the sufficiency of Scripture, and the necessity of sweet spiritual communion with the crucified and living Christ—these impulses that lie behind the CCEF ministries make it easy to commend them to everyone who loves the Church."

John Piper, Founder, desiringGod.org; Chancellor, Bethlehem College & Seminary

Christian Counseling & Educational Foundation
ccef.org

Also Available from Edward T. Welch

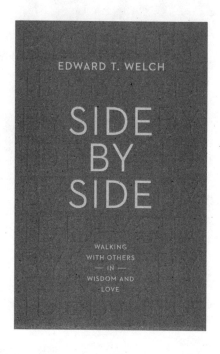

"I have come to rely on Welch for guidance and insight in better understanding the issues of the soul."
Bob Lepine, Co-Host, *FamilyLife Today*

"Welch has given us the wisdom that only comes from a heart shaped by the gospel and a deep compassion for people, generated by the love of Jesus."
Scotty Smith, Teacher in Residence, West End Community Church, Nashville, Tennessee

For more information, visit **crossway.org**.